UNSAID

The Poetic Mastery of

Lisa Lockhart

UNSAID
The Poetic Mastery of
Lisa Lockhart

Published By Glover Lane Press

Copyright ©2016 by Lisa Lockhart
Cover Design by Azaan Kamau

ISBN-13: 978-0692201787
ISBN-10: 0692201785

All rights reserved, including the right to reproduce or scan this book or portions thereof in any form whatsoever without the prior written permission of Lisa Lockhart and or Glover Lane Press except where permitted by law. Please do not participate in or encourage piracy of copyrighted materials in violation of author's rights.

Introduction

From the tender age of twelve years old I have had epilepsy. When the epilepsy started off I would have staring spells like I was daydreaming.

One day my mother was calling my name at the top of her lungs and I was just standing there on the front porch just staring into space. A few more incidents had occurred and my mother started to worry and think that my behavior may be something serious and she finally decided to take me to the emergency room and this was when I found out I had epilepsy.

Over the years I went from the staring seizures to the gran mal seizures where I would black out. Many times I wouldn't remember how the seizure would happen and how I ended up in the hospital. Back then I wouldn't take my medicine and would drink because I didn't want this condition and I felt angry on the inside.

Sometimes I even got picked on because of my condition. I was a bullied child!

I went through a lot of different medications to get the seizures under control.

In June 2013, I had a really bad one because I was stressed out and I had a really high fever. Even through all this I always had stories in my head and writing poetry and I even had hit rock bottom and there was nobody in my corner. This is when I realized the Lord blessed me with the gift of writing.

My family said I wasn't going to make it because of my condition. I didn't know any better so, I listen to them and stopped writing. God spoke to me and I started to write again and when I put that pen in my hand I felt complete. I am often called the shy one but I slowly began to come out of my shell and began to listen to my heart and I changed my mind set.

I went from having a negative attitude and second guessing myself to thinking positive and loving myself and being a fighter and not giving up on my dreams. I have been abused mentally and sexually and I am still standing and I am even stronger than ever. I am from Florida born and raised and lived here for thirty-nine years. Writing is my getaway and it frees my mind. In the years to come I will be a famous author and an entrepreneur. Live your dreams and make them come true and never give up and keep reaching for the stars.

Lisa LockHart

Unsaid

The Poetic Mastery of

Lisa Lockhart

Table of Contents

A Clear View 9
An Unopened Book 11
Moving On 13
Awaken 16
Naked Soul 18
Beautiful 20
I bleed 22
Mind Blowing 24
Missing You 26
Never 28
My Poetry 30
Outside Looking In 32
Pain 34
Scars on the Inside 36
The Meeting 38
Souls Connect 42
Thoughts in Between 44
Strung Out 46
Pretenders 47

Scars	49
I am Here	51
Hold You Down	55
Friends and Enemies	57
Disrespectful Wrongs	59
Dear Life	61
Alive	63
Doing Me	65
Missing	67
About Lisa Lockhart	71

A Clear View

Am I shocked?

Am I surprised?

Am I amazed?

Why am I surprised at what just happened

The one person who I thought loved and cared about me

The one person who said they loved me and that they were in love with me

And that they couldn't see their life without me

The one person I thought I could trust and the one person I thought would protect me

You lied to me over and over again you filled my head up with false hopes and dreams

Whispering all those words of sweet nothings and words of pure bliss were short lived it was only an act

You cheated on me with another and I was a fool to think that you were going to be faithful to me

I remember all those late night hang up calls from your other lover

I was being called stupid for being with you by my family and friends

You had groupies everywhere you had your own fan club going on

When I talked to you about how it made me feel you only ignored my feelings

What happened to the love that we once shared and what happened to all those precious memories

Are we just two lost souls trying to find our way back to each other?

Will we ever find our way back to each other or is this the end for us

An Unopened Book

As I am sitting here looking over the memories of my life

Like an unopened book that has never been opened or have never been read

Nobody knows what I am feeling on the inside

When you see me I am smiling on the outside and you think that I have it all

But in reality I am slowly dying on the inside

Like leeches eating away at a decayed body

I am wondering when this pain will stop

When I look in the mirror I see a stranger staring back at me

I see a reflection of a little girl just dying to be free but she feels trapped

As the tears roll down my face ever so gently I keep asking myself why over and over again

Will I ever have that fairytale happy ending that every woman dreams of?

Or am I destined to live in misery for a lifetime

Why can't people love and accept me for who and what I am

When will I stop being an outsider and being tossed aside like an old toy?

Will I ever see the beautiful soul that everybody else sees?

Or will I be held hostage in my own mind prison

Moving On

My mind is still spinning, I just can't wrap my mind around the situation just how it happened

As I walk around in a cloud of happiness pretending that everything is great

But deep down in my heart and soul I know that our love for each other has changed

I ask myself why I am still here in this loveless relationship, it's not getting better

Am I still here because I am in love with you or am I still here because it's the thought of being in love

Do you have some kind of voo-doo spell on me that keep me here with you?

My heart is telling me to leave but my mind is telling me that we should work it out

My idea of love and what it should be like is different from your idea of what love is

Your idea of love is putting your hands on me and not in an intimate or loving way

I always end up with bruises all over my body and I always have to cover them up

Every morning I look at myself in the mirror and I see black eyes and busted lips

If I don't want to make love you will just take it by force

When will I say enough is enough and that this is not what love is or what it should feel like?

As I sit here replaying the scene over and over in my head like a scene in a movie

What happened to the person that I fell in love with and wanted to spend the rest of my life with?

My mind, body, and soul is tired of all the pain and suffering that you are causing

At one point I thought that our souls were connected for life and that we would never part

Have we reached the end of the road or are you willing to change to make a new beginning

The love I had for you is dead and I have to set you free and start working on the new me

Awaken

Thank you for coming into my life

And showing me what real love feels like

And showing me what true passion looks and feels like

As I sit here thinking of you it instantly brings a smile to my face and it makes my heart flutter

Just the mere thought of hearing your voice sends chills through my body

I am always asking myself where you have been all my life when I was on a journey looking for love

Finding you is like finding the world's most precious gem

Knowing you has awaken something deep inside my soul that was once dead and lifeless

Is now awaken and is full of life and passion

The connection we have is so sacred and bonded and it's unbreakable

Our souls are forever intertwined and we will always be as one

Naked Soul

As she closes her eyes she can still see what happened to her

He came into her room like he had did every night

And the closer he got to her the more she could smell his bad alcoholic breath

Through slurred words he told her that he just had to have her because she was so beautiful

As he laid his heavy frame on her petite frame and she tried to push him off of her but he was too heavy

He ripped off all her clothes and she could feel his rough callused hands all over her body

To make the time go by she looked out her bedroom window she pretended to be somewhere else

After he was done the tears was running down her eyes and he had left her room

Opening her eyes she still felt nasty and dirty on the inside and out

Because of what happen to her she never gave herself completely to anyone

And she was scared and damage for life

Beautiful

When I look in the mirror

Who do I see?

I see the hair

I see the make-up and the manicured nails

I see the beautiful smile that could melt the coldest heart

I see the nice clothes and shoes

I see the nice car that people only fanaticize about

I see the nice home that that people only dream about out having

I stand before this mirror with a naked body and a naked soul

Like an illusion on a deserted island everything isn't always what it seems

I am the perfect illusion of what you want to see

When you see me on the street you think I can have any and everything I desire

But when I close my eyes I see an innocent soul that's looking for love, trust, and respect

I am beautiful on the outside but I feel ugly on the inside

When you see me you call me beautiful and I ask myself why I am beautiful to you

Am I beautiful because of what you see on the outside instead of what's on the inside?

Am I beautiful because of my body type or am I beautiful because of the color of my skin

Am I beautiful because of what I sound like when you hear me speak for the first time?

If I took away all the make-up and all the materialistic things will I still be beautiful to you

I bleed

When my heart is hurting and it is broken from a lover's betrayal

I bleed

When I have been lied to and cheated on

I bleed

When I have been talked about behind my back

I bleed

When my friends leave me by the waste side and left me high and dry

I bleed

When my naïve ears are filled with broken promises and deceit

I bleed

When I hit rock bottom and my back is against the wall

I bleed

When my thoughts take over and I am on an adventure in the world of the unknown

I let my pen bleed on the pages of my pad as my emotions fill the pages

So my message can be read or even heard

My pen bleeds for a lifetime and last for an eternity

Mind Blowing

I thought that I had finally found happiness and joy but all that came to an end

My world was shattered when I saw you in the arms of another and I was speechless

The heartbreaking scene was a shock to me because by the looks of things you were happy

You had this special kind of glow in your eyes and I remember when you use to give me that same glow

As I stand here and think where did our love go wrong and when did you stop loving me

Was I the only one in the relationship that was still in love or was I living in a fantasy world

What made you go astray was it my nagging you all the time or was it me not trusting you enough

Like the wind blowing a piece of paper in a deserted town and I was blown away by this discovery

With mixed feelings that I have for you part of me is angry and another part is relieved

Our souls are no longer connected and we are two souls that are wondering aimlessly in space

Our sad end is bittersweet but our new beginning is refreshing and we both have moved on

Missing You

As I sit here eyes closed I can see your beautiful smile and your beautiful face

Looking back over the memories flowing back to me like an endless stream

I miss the way you smiled when you were proud of something or someone or when you were surprised

I miss hearing the way you laughed when you thought something was funny

I miss your carefree spirit that you had before the cloud of darkness took over your body and soul

As I open my tear stained eyes I can still feel the tears gently kissing my cheeks

I miss you more and more every day with every passing moment

I know that you are totally free of all the pain and suffering while you were here on earth

But now you are with God and his beautiful angels, now you have no worries or cares

Until we are together again in heaven I will hold all those precious moments close to my heart

I will love you always and forever.

Never

Never had I thought it would be you

Never had I thought that you would do it to me

Never had I thought that you would say those hurtful words to me that just ripped my heart into shreds

Never will I feel you touching me in the intimate way that you use to when we made love

Our bodies will never touch again and our souls will never connect again

Like a tiger craving for a hunger that can't be satisfied or fulfilled

As I close my tear stained eyes I can see you and I can feel you wrapping your arms around me

Your once loving arms are gently caressing my hot and hungry body

Like a virgin being touched and kissed for the very first time

I feel your soft lips kissing me gently all over my smooth chocolate body

Your lips then move gently towards my chocolate melons and it begins to turn me on

Your kisses feel like chocolate raindrops falling from the sky

Your soft lips gently caresses my hot body that makes me melt like frosting on a cake

As I slowly open my eyes I soon realize that those were only precious memories we once shared

Our once in paradise fairy tale is now just a distant memory and we will never be together again

My Poetry

I want my poetry to move you

I want my poetry to give you something you can feel

I want my poetry to leave you breathless

I want my poetry to make you sit back and think

I want my poetry to touch your soul

I want my poetry to give you passion

I want my poetry to be an obsession

I want my poetry to be a habit

I want my poetry to make love to your mind, body, and soul

I want my poetry to make you lose control

I want my poetry to send chills up and down your spine

I want my poetry to roll off your tongue

I want my poetry to make you want to slow dance

I want my poetry to keep you in a trance

I want my poetry to make you laugh

I want my poetry to make you cry

I want my poetry to make you never want to say goodbye

Outside Looking In

When you see me you think that I have it all just because I have a smile on my face

But underneath this beautiful smile is a lot of pain and hurt that is easily hidden

When people see me out on the street they always see this plastered smile on my face

And to an outsider looking in they think I don't have problems and heartache

I have had my share of heartaches. I have been cheated on numerous times

When I see a happy couple walking hand in hand and are so much in love, I just smile at them

In the back of my mind I want what everybody else wants and that's to find their true soul mate

Deep inside my heart is shattered like broken glass from a terrible accident

When I enter this dark place I call home its empty, and I have no one to greet me at the door

There are no late night calls from my lover asking me how my day was

I don't have a candle light dinner waiting for me when I get home or even have my bath ready

Like a deaf mute the silence is deafening and it instantly bring tears to my eyes

Will I ever find that special someone who will treat me like a queen that I know I am?

Pain

As I look out my window I see bodies being sold some are not even twenty years old

I see drive by's and I hear a mother's cry as her child lays lifeless on the ground

And she looks towards the sky screaming out why but like a deaf mute all you hear is silence

As the dark clouds begin to form in the sky feel like the world is in a cruel place

Stepping outside I see a battered woman with a black eye and a busted lip and she is selling her soul

As I look deep into her eyes I see fear and pain and she reminds me of a scared little girl

As her mind wonders to another place and she feels as though she is stuck in this place

The world is full of pain and it is cruel to people who can't be themselves without being judged

When all the pain in the world ends… everyone will be treated equal

Scars on the Inside

You said that I'm never going to make it, you said that I am nothing without you

But, I am nothing while I am with you. Your harsh words cut through my soul like a knife

You said I was to country. You said I wasn't pretty enough for you

When I didn't do what you wanted you would call me harsh and cruel names

As I look in the mirror I see a stranger staring back at me through a busted lip and a blackened eye

As I take a closer look at this stranger in the mirror she does seem somewhat familiar

The once strong, confident, and beautiful woman with the beautiful soul to match no longer exists

All that is left is a weak woman with a bruised broken spirit and a broken soul

I ask myself will my spirit ever be fixed, will my soul ever recover from the abuse

Who will pick up the pieces of my broken heart?

You say you love me, yet you raise your hand to me over and over again

You tell me how sorry you are and that I made you hit me, it's like a song on repeat

I ask myself why am I still here and why do I continue to put up with the abuse

I am like a coach on a football team, pumping myself up saying that you will change your ways

Will these scars on the inside ever heal on the outside?

The Meeting

I'm nervous about the situation

I'm stepping into unknown territory and I'm feeling a lot of friction between my thighs

I'm wearing a mask so no one will know my true identity

Looking around the room at strange faces the women were giving me fever and friction at the same time

All of a sudden a voice comes up from behind and whispered in my ear walk towards the door

 I will be right behind you the sound of this stranger's voice made my panties wet.

Walking towards the door turning the door knob ever so slowly, stepping inside the room I hear the door close behind me

Standing behind me you start kissing my neck mmmmmm......I moaned as you unzipped my dress

It fell to my ankles I stepped out of it. Your sexy soft lips begin kissing my neck

Putting an arch in my back I bent over letting you know I was ready

Kneeling down you pulled my purple laced thongs down with your teeth

As I stepped out of them you bent me over and spanked my ass cheeks

You started kissing and rubbing my ass cheeks

No friction between your fingers and my pussy

mmmmmmm.......daddy this shit feels good I moaned

You began to lick me from behind mmmmm... daddy I moaned a little louder

Unsnapping my bra from the front my breasts fell to my chest

Licking and sucking my nipples with your long lizard tongue was driving me crazy

Leading me to the bed I was horny and I started rubbing myself and licking my lips

mmmmm...baby that shit is turning me on you said

You started eating my sweet nectar

No friction was being made when your lizard tongue touched my fat clit

No friction from your strap as I got on top

I can ride it like a pro oooooh daddy right there I moaned loudly damn this shit feel so good

Going faster and faster back and forth I got louder and louder

I'm not gonna stop daddy it feels good to you daddy

No friction between my womanhood and your strap they

Fit together like a hand in glove both of our bodies were sweaty we came together

It was ecstasy that I never felt before

You ready for another round are you ready for me

Souls Connect

When I first heard your beautiful voice it instantly brought a smile to my face

I feel as though we have met before could be that we met in another time or in another place

From the moment that our lips touched for the first time I knew I was hooked

Like a drug addict with a bad habit I just can't seem to get enough of you

Baby you are my drug of choice and you send me on a natural high

When I look into those beautiful eyes of yours I am mesmerized every time I look at you

Every time I close my eyes I can smell your fresh cologne that tickles my nostrils

When I am in your presence I feel protected in those loving arms of yours

Baby you know me better than I know myself and our souls are as one

You tell me what I am thinking even before I say it

We were meant to be and our souls were meant to be connected for eternity

Thoughts in Between

Lying here in my bed surrounded by the darkness

I am surrounded by the quietness and it's just me and my thoughts

Closing my eyes I see pretty pictures of us. I thought you were the one for me

But yet once again I got played like a brand new guitar freshly brought out of the store

I came into this life with a naked soul along with a naked body

Sweet words and promises of friendships and love and they were never real from the start

Promises from so called friends are easily forgotten like yesterday's news

Am I that easily to forget and after all those times that I had your back

I was the only one in your corner and this is how you treat me

But, when I was down on my luck and needed a shoulder to lean on you weren't around

My spirit is broken and bruised but it can be fixed in time

I have been disrespected and have been called cruel names

I didn't love myself enough and I use to think it was true

But as I look towards the future and I know that I am destined for true success

And you can't hold me down anymore. I want to thank you for opening my eyes

Giving me a clear view of who you really are

Strung Out

It's been two weeks since the last time that we have seen each other but to me it seems like a lifetime

Baby you got me under your spell and all I want to do is just surrender to you

Baby I don't want anybody else's tongue to touch my body but yours

Listening to your sexy voice just stimulates my mind and does something to my soul

When I don't hear from you it drives me crazy and I can't even function right

Baby not hearing from you I feel like a drug addict that need their daily fix to survive

Baby what are you doing to me do you have some type of voodoo on me

Baby I am strung out over you and I can't be without you

Pretenders

You say that you are happy for me but deep down inside you wish that I would fail

You say you love me but in reality you hate me and you are jealous of me

You hate everything about me from the way that I talk to the way that I dress

You have my swag and you have my smile and you hate that I'm doing the things you can't

You talk behind my back and then smile in my face

You try to be me but the truth of the matter is you will never be me

You are thirsty for attention and it makes you feel a certain type of way, I don't have to do that

You pretend like you want to see me succeed and you always give me a fake smile

You talk behind my back and when I come around you pretend that you have my back

Well why you are busy hating on me I'll be reaching for the top and I will leave you in the dust

Scars

These scars that I have run deep in my soul like a flowing river

You said that you loved me but yet you lied to me with your broken promises

Like being robbed you took something so precious and sacred that I can never get back

You stole my heart, mind, and sprit that I can never get back

Because of the damage you have caused I am always suspicious of others and my guard is always up

I always keep others after you at arm's length because the scars are still there

Like an open wound that needs to heal I have my heart guarded

I ask myself when all the pain and suffering stop, will I move on with my life

As I close my eyes I can still see you and I can still smell your enticing scent underneath my nose

As I open my eyes I can feel the tears rolling down my face and I realized that the pain is still fresh

As I stand before you it's like I am looking at a stranger, meeting you for the first time

No matter how many times you say that you are sorry it doesn't matter because the damage is done

I gave you all of me and you just took me for granted and you cut my heart into shreds

These scars that I have are still fresh. They will heal one day and maybe I will love again

Love is like a stranger to my heart and I am afraid to let anyone get close to me again

I am Here

You said that I would never make it but look at me now

You said to get my head out of the clouds because I am living in a fantasy world

You said that no one would ever love or care about me or even take me serious

But look at me now

You said nothing comes to a dreamer but disappointment and failure but you were wrong

You said that I am never going to leave my dead end job and that I was stuck there for the rest of my life

But as I see the shock and surprised look on your face it makes me feel good on the inside

Why the gas face what you thought I was just going to give up and just listen to you

You said people like me are only good for stealing, selling, and slanging

But look at me now I proved you wrong of your sick and twisted stereo typing

Don't judge me unless you know me personally

Don't judge me unless you have walked a mile in my shoes and have been where I have been

I may have hit rock bottom but I am on my way to the top and I say this to you I am here so get ready

Judge Me Not

Why do you judge me?

Am I a thief just because of the color of my skin and what type of clothes I am wearing?

Am I dumb and slow just because I didn't finish my education and I didn't graduate

Just because I don't have the book knowledge does that mean that I don't deserve that job position?

When I smile at you does that mean that I trust you and I will tell you all of my business?

Just because I am smiling on the outside doesn't mean that I am happy on the inside

Behind closed doors it is a different story and I am not smiling at all

I just got laid off from my job and I can't provide for my family

I have bills that are still rolling in. I am getting deeper and deeper in debt

I am in danger of getting evicted soon if I can't find a job real soon

My children wear hand me down clothes and shoes because I can't buy the latest style

Just because I don't show off my assets doesn't make me less of a woman that needs love

Just because I am quiet that doesn't mean that I think that I am better than you

Never judge a book by its cover if you have never even opened the book

Hold You Down

When I first laid my eyes on you I knew that you were special

I knew that I had to have you and that I wanted you in my life

But your heart wasn't in it your heart belonged to another

All those nights of hearing your smooth and sexy voice and you only spoke of her and how she hurt you

In my mind and in my soul I wanted you in every way and I knew I would never hurt you

I would never treat you like an old broken down car and I would cherish you

I would be that mechanic that would fix what is broken

I would cherish you like you were a one of kind necklace and I would never take it off

Baby all that I am asking is that you give me once chance and I would treat you like a king

I would be there for you through thick and thin and I would hold you down

I would be there for you through the good and bad times and baby I got your back

Baby let me hold you down for life

Friends and Enemies

As I climb up this mountain called life I have had a long and hard journey

People who say that they are your friends and that they will always be there for you

They turn out to be your enemies and these so called friends stab you in your back

The closer and closer I get to the top of the mountain there is always an obstacle that faces me

All types of snakes and leeches that surround my feet and try to bring me down

And all the fake smiles from family and friends surround me

When I make it to the top don't pretend that you were by my side all the time

Don't think that I will ever forget all those harsh and cruel words you said to me

And all those times you called me stupid, dumb, and ugly will always be stuck in the back of my mind

I don't want to hear how sorry you are and how much you want me back in your life

Looking back I was blinded by your fake love you had for me. I see you for who and what you are

The love and respect I had for you is long gone. Love don't live here anymore

Disrespectful Wrongs

Am I wrong for wanting to be loved?

Am I wrong for wanting to be free to love without feeling like the walls are closing in on me?

To an outsider looking in I seem to be happy and have it all

My smile can be deceiving, I have many people fooled by this plastered smile on my face

When I walk out into this cruel world I am judged by strangers for being the real me

As we walk hand in hand I see the frowns and the shaking of the heads and I hear the whispers

Why am I judged by society for loving someone just like me?

Why am I judged by my clothes and what I look like and who I want to be with?

Why do society make a big deal because we want to be treated equal and have the same rights

Why am I called cruel names because I am not attracted to you?

Why am I a victim of a hate crime because you have a sick phobia about me?

I have been raped and beaten and even killed because of your phobia you have towards me

When will the disrespect end and the respect begin?

Dear Life

You have been a teacher to me over the years and you continue to teach me

You have taught me life lessons and I begin to ask myself why I am here on this earth

You have brought me good and bad lovers that have brought me joy and pain

You have taken precious love ones away from me who I held close to my heart

But as years passed I soon began to realized that it was your plan to make me a stronger person

Coming into this world I knew I was different

I knew I was special and that I was like no other and you made me stronger

You made me more confident about myself

The hard and tough lessons you have placed before me I now know they were only a test

I have been abused mentally and physically but I am still standing. I have weathered the storm

I have had my precious jewels taken away from me, this has made me have trust issues

My insecurities that I have has kept people at arm's length

I have become a stranger to happiness and joy and I am the poster child of heartache and pain

You have taught me lessons that I didn't want to learn. You forced me to open my eyes

I now understand why you brought me through all of these hard trials and tribulations

You still have more to teach me and class is still in session

Alive

Like sleeping beauty I am awake baby

I see you baby I feel you baby

I want you baby

I need you baby

I have a hunger craving that only you can satisfy

Your lips are my one desire

There is no cure for my addiction that can be filled by a pharmacy or a drug store

The only cure for my addiction is you baby

The cure is your touch, your lips, your voice and your heart

My heart that was once broken is now fixed

Baby my pain is your pain and my happiness is your happiness

Baby you know me better than I know my own self

Baby there is something about you that just makes me want to surrender to you

I am like a bird that's been in a cage and trapped for so long

The cage door has finally opened and baby I am free to spread my once broken wings

I am no longer a prisoner of my own heart and soul

These feeling I have are strange but at the same time they are familiar

Finally, I can love and care without no restraints to hold me down

Baby you are the wind beneath my wings and I can fly free

I am alive carefree and I can be me

Doing Me

Finally I have opened my eyes I was once blind but now I see

Finally I am putting myself first instead of putting other people wants and needs ahead of my own

No more stealing my dreams like a thief in the night

No more sleepless nights and tear stained eyes from all the pain and deceit from love ones

No more being fooled by your beautiful lies and broken promises

No more believing and settling for your beautiful words that fall from those beautiful lips of yours

No more worrying about what other people think or say about me

No more fairy tale friends that promise to stand by my side through thick and thin

I am doing me and I am letting go of the past and holding on to present

I am getting ready for my bright and beautiful future. It's my time to shine

I am like a bird that soars in the wind and I am reaching for the stars

Look out world and get ready for me because I am taking over. I am doing me!

Missing

Am I wrong for not fighting for our relationship?

Am I wrong to not continue to love you like I once did?

Should I just follow my mind instead of my heart?

Should I tell you how I really feel or should I just keep it all bottled up on the inside?

When will the tears stop falling on my pillow each and every night?

Will I ever smile again or will I always have a permanent frown on my beautiful face

When will my pure heart stop breaking every time I hear your voice?

When will my heart and soul make beautiful music together again?

Will my heart always be broken for life?

Unsaid

The emptiness is still there and I feel like something is missing

You had been on my mind for the longest time, so I tried calling you but I got no response

When I got the news that God had called you home my whole world was shattered.

Like a boxer punching his opponent in the stomach I fell to my knees

You were my first love, you were my everything. I am going to miss you like crazy

As I lay here the tears keep running down my face, a smile appears on my face

I begin to think of all the happy times we had once shared. I will always cherish those precious times

I am going to miss you saying baby I love you. I am going to miss you saying how much you miss me

I am going to miss you holding me in your loving arms and never letting me go

I am going to miss all those beautiful kisses you gave me every night and day

I am going to miss all the late night talks on the phone until both of us fell asleep

I know that you're not in pain anymore and you're not suffering anymore

I know in my heart that we will be together again in heaven

Like the sun in the sky I know that you are smiling down on me

"God spoke to me and I started to write again! When I put that pen in my hand I felt complete"
Lisa Lockhart

About Lisa Lockhart

Author Lisa Lockhart writes beyond the pain as she struggles with epilepsy. As a child she was angered by her illness, and also tormented by bullies.

She went into a shell.

After a severe grand mal seizure back in 2013, her family had given up thinking she wasn't going to live! That night Spirit told Lisa that it wasn't her time and she still had work to do!

According to Lisa, she changed her mind set, and went from having a negative attitude!

She started writing through the pain!

Lisa began to really love herself, and have unwavering faith in herself, and became a warrior in the face of illness, mental and sexual abuse!

Today Lisa Lockhart is a living testament that no matter what life has given you, you too can reach for the stars!

Visit Lisa on Facebook!

www.ingramcontent.com/pod-product-compliance
Lightning Source LLC
LaVergne TN
LVHW051158080426
835508LV00021B/2687